Chapter 1: Introduction to Employee Cost Management

Understanding Employee Costs

Understanding employee costs is a multifaceted challenge that directly impacts the financial health of any organization. It encompasses not just salaries and wages but also a range of expenses including benefits, training, and the resources required to maintain a productive workforce. Recognizing the full spectrum of these costs enables businesses to implement strategies that enhance productivity while simultaneously reducing expenses. This understanding is crucial for entrepreneurs aiming to streamline their operations and improve their bottom line.

In the context of remote work, employee costs take on new dimensions. Organizations must evaluate how remote work affects expenditures such as technology, office supplies, and utilities. While remote work can lead to savings on physical office space, it may also necessitate investments in digital tools and platforms to support collaboration and communication. By analyzing these costs carefully, businesses can optimize their remote work strategies, ensuring that they are not only saving money but also maintaining or improving employee productivity.

Training and development represent another significant area of employee costs that can yield high returns on investment when managed effectively. The costs associated with onboarding new employees, continuous learning, and skill enhancement must be weighed against the potential benefits of a well-trained workforce. A strategic approach to employee development can lead to increased engagement, higher retention rates, and ultimately, improved performance metrics. Companies that prioritize training often find that the initial expenses are outweighed by the long-term advantages of having a more competent and motivated workforce.

Technology solutions play a pivotal role in managing employee costs. By investing in systems that streamline operations, track performance metrics, and facilitate communication, organizations can gain insights into where costs can be reduced. Automation and data analytics can help identify inefficiencies in staffing, project management, and resource allocation. This allows businesses to make informed decisions about outsourcing versus in-house staffing strategies, ensuring that each dollar spent contributes effectively to overall organizational goals.

Creating a culture of cost awareness among employees is essential for fostering an environment where everyone is invested in managing expenses. When employees understand the financial implications of their actions, they are more likely to engage in practices that align with the company's cost management objectives. Flexible work arrangements and a focus on employee engagement can further enhance this culture, as they provide employees with the autonomy to contribute to cost-saving initiatives while maintaining job satisfaction. By embedding cost awareness into the company ethos, businesses can achieve sustainable financial health and drive long-term success.

Importance of Cost Management in Today's Business Landscape

In today's fast-paced business environment, effective cost management has become a crucial pillar for sustainable growth and competitiveness. Companies face a myriad of challenges that demand not only strategic foresight but also a meticulous approach to managing expenses. With the rise of remote work, organizations must navigate new cost structures while ensuring that productivity remains high. This dual focus on enhancing performance and reducing expenses is essential for businesses aiming to thrive in an increasingly complex landscape.

The importance of cost management is particularly evident in the context of employee training and development. Investing in workforce skill enhancement is vital, yet organizations must measure the return on investment (ROI) of these initiatives carefully. By analyzing the outcomes of training programs, businesses can allocate resources more effectively, ensuring that both employee competencies and financial health are optimized. This strategic alignment not only enhances employee capabilities but also contributes to lower turnover rates and increased overall productivity.

Technology solutions play a pivotal role in modern cost management strategies. The integration of advanced tools and software enables organizations to streamline processes, automate repetitive tasks, and gain insights through data analytics. These innovations lead to reduced operational costs and improved decision-making capabilities. By leveraging technology, businesses can track performance metrics that inform cost efficiency, allowing for real-time adjustments that optimize resource allocation and drive better financial outcomes.

The choice between outsourcing and in-house staffing is another critical aspect of cost management. Companies must weigh the benefits of flexibility and specialization against the potential for higher long-term costs associated with outsourcing. A thorough analysis of each approach's financial implications helps businesses identify the most cost-effective solutions while maintaining quality and performance standards. Additionally, establishing a culture of cost awareness among employees can further enhance the effectiveness of these strategies, empowering teams to contribute to overall financial health.

Finally, flexible work arrangements have emerged as a significant factor in workforce planning and budgeting techniques. Organizations that embrace flexibility often find that it leads to increased employee engagement and retention, translating into lower recruitment and training costs. However, careful financial analysis is necessary to understand the broader impact of these arrangements. By fostering an environment that prioritizes both employee well-being and cost efficiency, businesses can cultivate a motivated workforce that drives success in today's dynamic market.

Overview of Strategies for Success

Strategies for success in employee cost management require a multifaceted approach that considers the diverse elements impacting an organization's financial health. One of the critical areas to address is enhancing productivity while simultaneously reducing expenses. Businesses can achieve this by implementing streamlined processes that optimize workflows and minimize waste. By fostering a culture of efficiency, organizations can empower employees to identify cost-saving opportunities, leading to improved performance and lower operational costs. This proactive approach not only enhances productivity but also cultivates a sense of ownership among employees, contributing to long-term success.

Remote work has become a pivotal consideration for many businesses, particularly in optimizing costs associated with employee management. Companies can leverage technology to facilitate remote work arrangements that reduce overhead expenses, such as office space and utilities. Additionally, organizations should focus on establishing clear communication channels and performance metrics that align remote employees with corporate goals. By investing in the right tools and processes, businesses can ensure that remote work contributes positively to cost management while maintaining employee engagement and productivity.

Employee training and development represent another crucial strategy for maximizing return on investment (ROI) in workforce development. By prioritizing ongoing education and skill enhancement, organizations can equip their employees with the tools necessary to adapt to changing market demands. This investment not only increases employee satisfaction and retention but also enhances overall productivity. Furthermore, businesses should regularly assess the effectiveness of training programs to ensure they deliver tangible benefits, helping to justify the associated costs and align with broader financial goals.

Technology solutions play an integral role in optimizing cost management strategies. Implementing advanced software and tools can streamline various processes, from payroll and benefits administration to performance tracking and analytics. By utilizing data-driven insights, organizations can make informed decisions that enhance efficiency and reduce unnecessary expenditures. Furthermore, adopting technology solutions encourages a culture of innovation among employees, who can leverage these tools to improve their workflows and contribute to the company's bottom line.

Finally, cultivating a culture of cost awareness among employees is essential for sustainable success in cost management. Encouraging open discussions about financial responsibilities and cost-saving initiatives fosters a sense of collective ownership. Organizations should involve employees in budget planning and performance evaluations, creating an environment where everyone is aligned with the company's financial objectives. By integrating cost awareness into the organizational culture, businesses can ensure that all employees are engaged in identifying opportunities for improvement, ultimately leading to a more efficient and financially stable operation.

Chapter 2: Enhancing Productivity While Reducing Expenses

Identifying Key Productivity Metrics

Identifying key productivity metrics is essential for businesses seeking to enhance operational efficiency while managing employee costs. Productivity metrics provide quantifiable data that can help organizations assess performance, streamline processes, and implement strategies that align with their cost management goals. By focusing on the right metrics, businesses can uncover insights that drive decision-making and foster a culture of continuous improvement.

One of the most critical productivity metrics is output per employee, which measures the total output produced relative to the number of employees. This metric allows organizations to evaluate workforce performance and identify high-performing teams or individuals. By comparing output per employee across different departments or project teams, businesses can pinpoint areas that require additional training, support, or resources, ultimately leading to more efficient employee cost management.

Another important metric to consider is the employee engagement score, which reflects how motivated and committed employees are to their work. High engagement levels often correlate with increased productivity and lower employee turnover, which can significantly reduce recruitment and training costs. Businesses can measure engagement through surveys or feedback mechanisms, using the data to develop targeted strategies that enhance employee satisfaction and retention while optimizing costs associated with hiring and onboarding.

Additionally, technology solutions play a vital role in enhancing productivity metrics. Tools that facilitate remote work, project management, and communication can help organizations streamline operations and improve collaboration among teams. By tracking technology usage and assessing its impact on productivity, businesses can identify areas where additional investment may be warranted or where cost-saving measures can be applied without compromising performance.

Finally, performance metrics related to training and development ROI are crucial for understanding the effectiveness of employee investment. By measuring the impact of training programs on productivity, businesses can make informed decisions about future training initiatives and allocate resources more efficiently. This analysis not only helps in justifying training costs but also ensures that employee development efforts align with overall productivity goals, creating a more competent and cost-effective workforce.

Streamlining Work Processes

Streamlining work processes is crucial for businesses aiming to enhance productivity while simultaneously reducing costs. One effective approach involves mapping out existing workflows to identify bottlenecks and areas for improvement. By analyzing each step in a process, organizations can eliminate redundancies, streamline communication, and ensure that resources are allocated efficiently. This not only saves time but also minimizes the likelihood of errors, which can lead to increased costs. Adopting lean methodologies can be beneficial, as they focus on maximizing value while reducing waste, aligning perfectly with the goal of efficient employee cost management.

In the context of remote work, streamlining processes becomes even more essential. As organizations transition to hybrid or fully remote models, it is vital to leverage technology that facilitates seamless collaboration and communication among team members. Tools such as project management software and collaborative platforms help to maintain clarity and accountability, ensuring that employees remain productive regardless of their location. Additionally, establishing clear guidelines for remote work can prevent miscommunication and enhance workflow efficiency, ultimately leading to cost savings in operational expenses.

Training and development play a significant role in streamlining work processes. By investing in employee skills, organizations can improve performance and reduce the time it takes to complete tasks. Implementing targeted training programs that focus on efficiency and cost management can yield a high return on investment. Employees equipped with the right skills are more likely to identify and address inefficiencies within their roles. Moreover, fostering a culture of continuous learning encourages innovation and adaptability, which are vital for maintaining competitiveness in a changing business landscape.

Technology solutions are indispensable for optimizing cost management strategies. Automation tools can significantly reduce the time spent on repetitive tasks, freeing employees to focus on higher-value activities. By integrating artificial intelligence and machine learning into operations, businesses can enhance decision-making processes and resource allocation. Furthermore, data analytics can provide insights into employee performance and cost metrics, enabling organizations to make informed choices about workforce management and budgeting. This technological integration not only streamlines processes but also contributes to long-term financial sustainability.

Finally, establishing performance metrics is essential for measuring the effectiveness of streamlined work processes. By setting clear goals and regularly assessing outcomes, organizations can identify areas that require further optimization. Moreover, engaging employees in this process fosters a culture of cost awareness, encouraging them to take ownership of their contributions to efficiency. By aligning individual performance with overall business objectives, companies can enhance employee engagement and retention while effectively managing costs. Striking the right balance between operational efficiency and employee satisfaction is the key to achieving sustainable success in today's competitive landscape.

Implementing Time Management Practices

Implementing effective time management practices is essential for businesses aiming to enhance productivity while simultaneously reducing costs. Time is a finite resource, and its efficient allocation can significantly impact overall operational effectiveness. To streamline processes, companies should adopt systematic approaches that enable employees to prioritize tasks, set realistic deadlines, and utilize tools that foster collaboration and accountability. This practice not only improves individual performance but also contributes to the organization's bottom line by minimizing wasted hours and increasing output.

One of the most impactful strategies for time management is the establishment of clear performance metrics. These metrics allow businesses to identify areas where employees excel and where improvements are necessary. By regularly reviewing these indicators, management can provide targeted feedback and training opportunities that align with organizational goals. Additionally, integrating technology solutions such as project management software can facilitate better scheduling and task delegation, ensuring that team members remain focused on high-priority projects and deadlines.

Remote work presents unique challenges and opportunities in time management. Employers must implement policies that encourage effective communication and collaboration among remote teams. Regular check-ins and the use of digital tools can help track progress and foster a sense of accountability. Furthermore, providing training on best practices for remote work can enhance employees' ability to manage their time effectively, ultimately leading to increased productivity and reduced operational costs associated with remote work environments.

Employee training and development must also be viewed through the lens of time management. Investing in skill development equips employees with the tools they need to work more efficiently and effectively. Training programs should include components on time management techniques and the use of technology that can streamline tasks. By enhancing employees' abilities to manage their time, organizations can see a measurable return on investment, not only in terms of productivity but also in employee satisfaction and retention.

Finally, fostering a culture of cost awareness and time efficiency among employees is crucial. This can be achieved by engaging staff in discussions around the importance of time management and its impact on the company's financial health. Encouraging employees to share best practices and success stories related to effective time management can create an environment where everyone feels responsible for optimizing both their time and the organization's resources. This cultural shift not only enhances individual and team performance but also reinforces the organization's commitment to efficiency and cost management, ultimately leading to sustained success.

Chapter 3: Remote Work Cost Optimization

Analyzing Remote Work Expenses

Analyzing remote work expenses is crucial for businesses seeking to optimize their cost management strategies. As organizations increasingly embrace flexible work arrangements, understanding the financial implications of remote work becomes paramount. Remote work can lead to noticeable cost savings, such as reduced overhead expenses associated with physical office spaces. However, it also introduces new expenditures, including technology investments, communication tools, and home office stipends. A comprehensive analysis of these expenses allows businesses to identify areas where they can cut costs while maintaining productivity and employee satisfaction.

When assessing remote work expenses, it is essential to categorize costs into direct and indirect expenditures. Direct expenses include items like software subscriptions, hardware provisions, and internet reimbursements, which are easily quantifiable. Indirect expenses, on the other hand, encompass factors such as the potential decline in team cohesion and the associated costs of employee engagement initiatives. By distinguishing between these categories, organizations can develop a clearer picture of their overall financial commitment to remote work, enabling more accurate budgeting and forecasting.

Moreover, leveraging technology solutions plays a significant role in managing remote work expenses effectively. Investing in collaborative tools and project management software can streamline workflows and enhance communication among remote teams. While these technologies may require upfront investments, they often lead to long-term savings by improving efficiency and reducing the time spent on administrative tasks. Organizations should conduct a cost-benefit analysis to ensure that the technology solutions they implement provide a favorable return on investment, contributing positively to their bottom line.

Another critical aspect of analyzing remote work expenses is evaluating the ROI of employee training and development within a remote context. As employees navigate new tools and methodologies in a remote setting, targeted training programs can enhance their productivity and engagement. However, these programs also incur costs, which must be weighed against the potential benefits. By measuring performance metrics before and after training initiatives, businesses can assess the effectiveness of their investments and adjust their strategies accordingly to optimize costs and outcomes.

Finally, fostering a culture of cost awareness among employees is essential for successful remote work expense management. When team members understand the financial implications of their actions, they are more likely to adopt practices that contribute to cost efficiency. Encouraging open discussions about expenses, providing resources for financial literacy, and recognizing individuals who exemplify cost-conscious behavior can create an environment where every employee feels responsible for the organization's financial health. This holistic approach not only optimizes remote work expenses but also enhances employee engagement and retention, fostering a sustainable and productive remote workforce.

Tools for Remote Work Efficiency

Tools for remote work efficiency are crucial in today's business landscape, particularly for organizations that aim to enhance productivity while managing costs effectively. The right tools can significantly streamline processes, foster collaboration, and improve communication among remote teams. By leveraging technology, businesses can not only maintain operational effectiveness but also reduce overhead costs associated with traditional office environments. This subchapter explores various tools that contribute to remote work efficiency, focusing on their functionalities and benefits.

One essential category of tools is project management software. Solutions like Trello, Asana, and Monday.com enable teams to organize tasks, set deadlines, and track progress in real-time. These platforms enhance transparency and accountability, allowing team members to understand their roles and responsibilities clearly. By using project management tools, companies can minimize miscommunication and ensure that projects stay on track, ultimately leading to better resource allocation and cost management.

Communication tools are another cornerstone of remote work efficiency. Platforms such as Slack, Microsoft Teams, and Zoom facilitate seamless interaction among team members, regardless of their physical location. Effective communication is vital for maintaining team cohesion and ensuring that everyone is aligned with company objectives. Furthermore, these tools often come with features that allow for file sharing, video conferencing, and instant messaging, which can reduce the need for travel and in-person meetings, thus saving costs.

Employee training and development can also benefit from remote work tools. Learning management systems (LMS) like Moodle and Coursera for Business provide employees with access to training materials and courses from anywhere. This not only enhances employee skills but also ensures a higher return on investment in training initiatives. By integrating training into the remote work framework, organizations can foster a culture of continuous learning while controlling expenses associated with traditional training methods.

Finally, data analytics tools play a pivotal role in measuring and optimizing performance metrics related to cost efficiency. Tools such as Tableau and Google Analytics enable businesses to track various performance indicators, including productivity levels and employee engagement. By analyzing this data, organizations can make informed decisions regarding workforce planning and budgeting. Understanding how remote work impacts performance can lead to more effective strategies for cost management and employee retention, ultimately contributing to a culture of cost awareness within the organization.

Best Practices for Reducing Remote Work Costs

When it comes to reducing costs associated with remote work, businesses should prioritize establishing clear communication strategies. Effective communication channels, such as dedicated team messaging platforms and regular video meetings, can minimize misunderstandings and streamline project management. By ensuring that all employees are aligned with company goals and project expectations, organizations can enhance productivity and reduce time lost to miscommunication. Furthermore, establishing guidelines for communication frequency and response times fosters a culture of accountability and efficiency, which is essential for remote teams.

Another critical aspect of cost reduction in remote work is the strategic use of technology. Investing in the right tools can significantly impact productivity while managing expenses. Cloud-based project management software, for instance, allows teams to collaborate seamlessly regardless of their location. Additionally, leveraging automation tools can reduce the time employees spend on repetitive tasks, thereby increasing their capacity for more value-added activities. By carefully evaluating technology solutions, businesses can find cost-effective alternatives that enhance operational efficiency without incurring unnecessary expenditures.

Employee training and development also play a vital role in optimizing remote work costs. Organizations should focus on providing targeted training that enhances employee skills relevant to remote work environments. This can include training on digital communication tools, time management, and self-motivation techniques. By investing in the professional growth of remote employees, companies can improve job satisfaction, which in turn boosts retention rates and reduces turnover costs. Enhanced skills lead to increased productivity, making the investment in training a strategic move for long-term cost management.

In addition to training, businesses should conduct regular performance metrics evaluations to identify areas for improvement within remote teams. By establishing key performance indicators (KPIs) related to productivity and cost efficiency, organizations can ensure that remote employees are meeting expectations. This data-driven approach enables companies to make informed decisions about resource allocation, whether that means providing additional support for underperforming areas or reallocating funds to high-performing teams. Regular assessments of performance metrics contribute to a culture of continuous improvement and cost awareness among employees.

Finally, promoting a flexible work arrangement can lead to significant cost savings while enhancing employee satisfaction. By allowing employees to choose their work hours or locations, businesses can reduce overhead costs associated with maintaining physical office spaces. Additionally, flexible arrangements can lead to increased employee engagement, as workers appreciate the autonomy and work-life balance that comes with remote work. This engagement not only improves productivity but also reduces the financial impact of turnover, as satisfied employees are more likely to remain with the organization. Emphasizing flexible work options, therefore, is a strategic approach to reducing remote work costs while fostering a positive organizational culture.

Chapter 4: Employee Training and Development ROI

Measuring Training Effectiveness

Measuring training effectiveness is critical for organizations seeking to enhance productivity while minimizing expenses. In today's competitive landscape, especially with the rise of remote work, businesses need to ensure their training programs yield a substantial return on investment (ROI). This involves not only assessing the immediate outputs of training sessions but also evaluating their long-term impact on employee performance and organizational goals. By establishing clear metrics and benchmarks, organizations can gain insights into how effectively their training initiatives translate into improved employee capabilities and overall business performance.

One of the primary methods of measuring training effectiveness is through the application of performance metrics. These metrics can include pre- and post-training assessments, which provide quantifiable data on employee knowledge and skill improvement. Furthermore, organizations can track key performance indicators (KPIs) related to job performance, such as productivity rates, error reduction, and customer satisfaction scores. By correlating these metrics with training participation, businesses can identify trends and determine whether their initiatives are fostering the desired outcomes.

In addition to performance metrics, organizations should consider the financial implications of their training programs. This involves conducting a comprehensive cost-benefit analysis to evaluate the expenses associated with training against the benefits realized through enhanced employee performance. Factors to consider include reduced employee turnover, improved efficiency, and increased revenue generation. Understanding these financial dynamics allows businesses to make informed decisions on future training investments and to justify expenditures to stakeholders.

Employee feedback is another vital component of measuring training effectiveness. Surveys and interviews can provide qualitative insights into participants' perceptions of the training content, delivery methods, and relevance to their roles. Gathering this feedback helps identify areas for improvement and ensures that training programs align with employee needs and organizational objectives. Additionally, engaging employees in the evaluation process fosters a culture of continuous improvement and accountability, ultimately leading to higher engagement and retention rates.

Finally, the integration of technology solutions can enhance the measurement of training effectiveness. Learning management systems and analytics tools can track participation, engagement levels, and skill acquisition in real-time. These technologies facilitate a more dynamic approach to training evaluation, enabling organizations to adapt their strategies based on data-driven insights. By leveraging such tools, businesses can ensure that their training initiatives not only contribute to employee development but also align with broader goals of cost efficiency and productivity enhancement.

Aligning Training with Business Goals

Aligning training with business goals is a critical strategy for organizations seeking to enhance productivity while managing employee costs effectively. By ensuring that training initiatives directly support the overarching objectives of the business, companies can maximize the return on investment (ROI) associated with employee development. This alignment helps to create a workforce that is not only skilled but also strategically focused on the organization's mission, leading to improved performance and cost efficiency.

To begin with, businesses must clearly define their goals and objectives before implementing training programs. Understanding what the organization seeks to achieve—whether it be increased sales, improved customer service, or enhanced operational efficiency—sets the foundation for developing targeted training initiatives. By conducting a thorough needs assessment, organizations can identify skill gaps and training needs that align directly with these defined goals. This ensures that resources are allocated effectively and that training contributes meaningfully to the organization's strategic priorities.

Moreover, leveraging technology solutions can significantly enhance the alignment of training with business goals. E-learning platforms and data analytics tools allow businesses to track employee progress and performance in real-time, enabling a more agile approach to training. Companies can adapt their training programs based on performance metrics, ensuring that the content remains relevant and impactful. This not only streamlines the training process but also facilitates continuous improvement, as organizations can make data-driven decisions to refine their training strategies over time.

In addition to technology, fostering a culture of cost awareness among employees plays a vital role in aligning training with business objectives. When employees understand the financial implications of their work and how their performance contributes to the company's success, they are more likely to engage actively in training programs. Organizations should communicate the value of training in relation to business goals, emphasizing how skill development can lead to better performance and, ultimately, cost savings. This alignment not only enhances employee engagement but also reinforces the importance of training as a strategic investment.

Finally, evaluating the effectiveness of training programs through a robust ROI analysis is essential for ensuring ongoing alignment with business goals. Organizations should establish performance metrics that measure the impact of training on key business outcomes, such as productivity levels, cost reductions, and employee retention. Regular assessments will help identify successful training initiatives and those that require modification. By continuously aligning training with business objectives, organizations can build a high-performing workforce that drives efficiency and supports long-term success in managing employee costs.

Cost-Effective Training Solutions

Cost-effective training solutions are essential for businesses striving to enhance productivity while managing expenses. In the contemporary workplace, where remote work has become commonplace, organizations must adapt their training methods to optimize costs without sacrificing quality. Embracing technology-driven training solutions, such as online learning platforms and virtual workshops, can significantly reduce costs associated with traditional in-person training. These methods not only eliminate travel and accommodation expenses but also allow for scalability, enabling businesses to train more employees simultaneously.

Moreover, effective employee training should be aligned with the overall goals of the organization to maximize return on investment (ROI). By implementing performance metrics to assess the effectiveness of training programs, businesses can identify which initiatives yield the highest benefits and which may require adjustments. Metrics such as employee retention rates, productivity improvements, and the reduction of errors can provide valuable insights into the training's impact, guiding future investments in employee development.

Incorporating flexible work arrangements can further enhance the effectiveness of training solutions. Remote work provides employees with the opportunity to engage in training at their convenience, leading to better retention of information and skills. Organizations that offer asynchronous training options allow employees to learn at their own pace, accommodating varying schedules and learning styles. This flexibility not only contributes to a more engaged workforce but also reduces the financial impact associated with scheduling conflicts and lost productivity during traditional training sessions.

Outsourcing training programs can also be a cost-effective strategy for many organizations. By partnering with external training providers, businesses can access specialized expertise without the overhead costs of maintaining an in-house training team. This approach allows companies to focus on their core competencies while leveraging the knowledge of external experts to deliver high-quality training. Additionally, outsourcing can provide more diverse training options, catering to a broader range of employee needs and preferences.

Cultivating a culture of cost awareness among employees is vital for the long-term success of training initiatives. When employees understand the financial implications of their training and development, they are more likely to take ownership of their learning and apply new skills effectively. Encouraging open dialogue about training budgets and outcomes fosters a collaborative environment where employees feel empowered to contribute to cost-saving strategies. By integrating cost awareness into the training framework, organizations can ensure that every dollar spent on employee development translates into measurable improvements in productivity and overall business performance.

Chapter 5: Technology Solutions for Cost Management

Automation Tools for Cost Reduction

Automation tools have become essential in the quest for cost reduction within organizations. These tools can streamline processes, minimize human error, and ultimately lead to significant savings in employee costs. By automating repetitive tasks, businesses can allocate more resources toward strategic initiatives that drive growth. For example, automating payroll processes not only reduces the administrative burden but also enhances accuracy, ensuring employees receive their rightful compensation without delays. As businesses continue to adapt to a rapidly changing environment, the integration of automation tools becomes a critical component of efficient employee cost management.

One of the primary areas where automation can yield substantial cost savings is in employee training and development. Traditional training methods often come with high expenses, including travel costs, materials, and instructor fees. However, automation tools such as Learning Management Systems (LMS) can deliver training modules online, allowing employees to learn at their own pace and on their own schedules. This not only cuts down costs associated with in-person training but also enhances the return on investment for employee development by providing measurable outcomes and tracking progress more effectively.

In the context of remote work, automation tools facilitate seamless communication and collaboration, which are vital for maintaining productivity and minimizing operational costs. Platforms that integrate project management, time tracking, and communication tools can help teams stay aligned and focused, regardless of their physical location. By reducing the need for physical office spaces and associated overhead costs, businesses can leverage these tools to optimize their workforce while maintaining high levels of employee engagement and performance.

Additionally, automation tools can significantly impact benefits and compensation analysis. By utilizing software that analyzes employee data and compensation structures, organizations can identify disparities and inefficiencies in their benefits offerings. This data-driven approach allows businesses to make informed decisions about employee compensation, ensuring that they are competitive in the market while also managing costs. Furthermore, automating the benefits enrollment process can enhance the employee experience, reducing administrative burdens on HR departments and allowing them to focus on strategic initiatives rather than paperwork.

Finally, fostering a culture of cost awareness among employees is crucial for long-term success. Automation tools can support this effort by providing real-time data and analytics that empower employees to understand their impact on the organization's financial health. By encouraging employees to engage with these tools and promoting transparency in cost management, businesses can cultivate a workforce that is more mindful of expenses and invested in the organization's overall success. This cultural shift not only enhances cost efficiency but also drives employee retention and engagement, ultimately contributing to a more resilient and profitable organization.

Software for Tracking Employee Costs

In the realm of employee cost management, software solutions have emerged as indispensable tools for businesses aiming to optimize their expenditures while enhancing productivity. These software systems provide comprehensive tracking capabilities that allow organizations to monitor various employee-related costs, such as salaries, benefits, training expenditures, and even the financial implications of remote work arrangements. By leveraging technology, businesses can gain insights into where their resources are being allocated and identify areas for potential savings, thereby streamlining their operations and fostering a culture of cost awareness among employees.

One of the primary advantages of utilizing software for tracking employee costs is the ability to automate data collection and reporting processes. Traditional manual methods often lead to errors and inconsistencies that can obscure the true financial picture of a company's workforce. By implementing specialized software, businesses can ensure accurate tracking of expenses related to employee compensation, benefits, and development programs. This automation not only saves time but also enables more reliable forecasting and budgeting, allowing decision-makers to allocate resources more efficiently in line with organizational goals.

Additionally, these software solutions facilitate the analysis of return on investment (ROI) for employee training and development initiatives. By tracking the costs associated with training programs alongside performance metrics, businesses can assess the effectiveness of their investments in employee growth. This enables organizations to make informed decisions about which programs yield the best results and which may require reevaluation or discontinuation. Such insights are crucial in fostering a culture of continuous improvement and ensuring that employee development efforts align with overall business objectives.

For businesses embracing remote work, software for tracking employee costs is particularly beneficial. It can help organizations understand the unique financial implications of remote versus in-house staffing strategies. By analyzing costs associated with remote work setups, such as technology investments and home office stipends, companies can develop more effective flexible work arrangements that balance employee needs with financial sustainability. This capability is essential for organizations looking to optimize their workforce planning and budgeting techniques in a changing work environment.

Finally, the integration of cost-tracking software promotes employee engagement and retention by providing transparency in compensation and benefits analysis. When employees have access to clear data regarding how their contributions impact overall costs and performance metrics, they are more likely to feel valued and connected to the company's financial health. This transparency fosters a sense of ownership among employees, encouraging them to actively participate in cost-saving initiatives and reinforcing the importance of a collective effort towards efficient employee cost management. In conclusion, the strategic use of software for tracking employee costs is a vital element in enhancing productivity while reducing expenses across various business sectors.

Leveraging Data Analytics for Cost Management

Leveraging data analytics for cost management is an essential strategy for businesses seeking to enhance productivity while reducing expenses. In the context of employee cost management, data analytics provides valuable insights that can inform decision-making processes related to staffing, training, and compensation. By analyzing historical data, businesses can identify trends and patterns that reveal opportunities for cost savings and efficiency improvements. This proactive approach allows organizations to make informed choices that align with their financial goals while maintaining a focus on employee engagement and retention.

One of the primary areas where data analytics can significantly impact cost management is in remote work optimization. By gathering and analyzing data on employee productivity, engagement levels, and associated costs of remote work, businesses can gain a clearer picture of how to allocate resources effectively. Metrics such as time spent on tasks, communication frequency, and project completion rates can be analyzed to identify which remote work strategies yield the best results. This information enables companies to refine their remote work policies, ensuring they support employee productivity while minimizing unnecessary expenses.

In the realm of employee training and development, data analytics can be instrumental in assessing the return on investment (ROI) of various programs. By tracking employee performance before and after training initiatives, organizations can gather quantitative data that illustrates the effectiveness of their training efforts. This analysis empowers businesses to make data-driven decisions about which training programs are most beneficial and cost-effective. Furthermore, it allows for the identification of skill gaps within the workforce, enabling targeted training that not only enhances employee capabilities but also optimizes training budgets.

Technology solutions play a crucial role in facilitating data analytics for cost management. By investing in advanced analytics tools and software, organizations can streamline data collection and analysis processes. These technology solutions allow businesses to consolidate data from various sources, providing a comprehensive view of employee costs and performance metrics. With real-time data at their fingertips, decision-makers can quickly identify areas of concern and implement strategies that align with both cost management objectives and overall business goals.

Lastly, cultivating a culture of cost awareness among employees is vital for sustainable cost management. By leveraging data analytics, organizations can share insights with employees regarding the financial implications of their work. This transparency fosters a sense of ownership and accountability, encouraging employees to contribute to cost-saving initiatives. When employees understand how their roles impact the bottom line, they are more likely to engage in behaviors that promote efficiency and reduce costs. Ultimately, integrating data analytics into cost management strategies not only enhances operational effectiveness but also aligns employee goals with organizational financial objectives.

Chapter 6: Benefits and Compensation Analysis

Evaluating Employee Benefits Packages

Evaluating employee benefits packages is a critical component of effective cost management in any organization. As businesses strive to enhance productivity while simultaneously reducing expenses, the right benefits package can serve as a strategic tool to attract and retain top talent. This evaluation process involves not only analyzing the financial implications of various benefits but also understanding their impact on employee engagement and overall organizational culture. Companies must consider how benefits align with their strategic objectives, ensuring that the offerings are both appealing to employees and sustainable for the business.

To effectively evaluate employee benefits packages, organizations should conduct a comprehensive analysis of current offerings compared to industry standards. This benchmarking process provides insights into what competitors are providing, which can help identify gaps in the current package. It is essential to gather feedback from employees through surveys or focus groups to understand their preferences and needs better. This information helps businesses tailor their benefits to enhance satisfaction and retention, ultimately impacting productivity positively.

In the context of remote work cost optimization, evaluating benefits packages takes on additional dimensions. Companies must consider how traditional benefits translate into a remote work environment. For instance, benefits related to commuting or on-site amenities may need to be rethought. Additionally, offering stipends for home office setups or wellness programs that support mental health in a remote setting can demonstrate a commitment to employee well-being, leading to increased productivity and morale. The evaluation should encompass the effectiveness of these remote-specific benefits in supporting employees' work-life balance while also contributing to cost efficiency.

Furthermore, organizations should assess the return on investment (ROI) of employee training and development programs as part of their benefits evaluation. Investing in employee growth not only enhances skill sets but can also lead to improved performance metrics and cost efficiency. Effective training programs should be aligned with the organization's strategic goals, ensuring that employees are equipped to contribute to cost management initiatives. By measuring the impact of these programs on productivity and retention, businesses can make informed decisions about which benefits yield the highest returns.

Ultimately, fostering a culture of cost awareness among employees is essential in the evaluation of benefits packages. When employees understand the financial implications of their benefits and how they contribute to overall organizational success, they are more likely to engage with the offerings. This culture can be cultivated through transparent communication regarding the benefits package and its alignment with business objectives. By involving employees in the evaluation process, organizations not only enhance their understanding of the value of benefits but also promote a sense of ownership and accountability, which can lead to greater overall efficiency and cost management.

Strategies for Competitive Compensation

Competitive compensation is a critical factor in attracting and retaining top talent in today's dynamic business environment. For entrepreneurs, understanding and implementing effective compensation strategies can significantly enhance productivity while managing costs. It is essential to develop a compensation structure that not only meets the financial expectations of employees but also aligns with the company's budgetary constraints. By leveraging market research and industry benchmarks, businesses can create competitive salary packages that reflect the value of their employees while maintaining fiscal responsibility.

Incorporating flexible compensation options can also contribute to a more attractive employment package. Many employees now prioritize benefits that go beyond salary, such as remote work opportunities, wellness programs, and professional development funding. By offering a mix of traditional and non-traditional benefits, companies can appeal to a broader range of candidates. This approach not only enhances employee satisfaction and engagement but also helps in reducing turnover rates, ultimately resulting in lower recruitment and training costs.

Performance-based compensation is another effective strategy that aligns employee goals with organizational objectives. Implementing bonus structures or profit-sharing plans can motivate employees to perform at their best, directly impacting productivity and profitability. This method fosters a culture of accountability and can lead to higher employee engagement, as individuals feel that their contributions are directly tied to their financial rewards. Additionally, transparent communication about performance metrics and compensation structures can enhance trust and collaboration within teams.

Investing in employee training and development can yield significant returns when integrated into the compensation strategy. By offering opportunities for skill enhancement and career advancement, companies not only improve employee performance but also demonstrate a commitment to their workforce's growth. This investment can lead to increased loyalty and reduced turnover, which is particularly beneficial in times of economic uncertainty. Furthermore, employees who feel supported in their professional development are more likely to engage in innovation and contribute to cost-saving initiatives.

Finally, creating a culture of cost awareness among employees can significantly impact compensation strategies. When employees understand the financial implications of their work and the importance of cost management, they are more likely to align their efforts with the company's financial goals. Regular training sessions on financial literacy, budgeting, and cost-saving practices can empower employees to contribute to organizational efficiency. By fostering this mindset, businesses can not only streamline compensation expenses but also cultivate a more engaged and responsible workforce, ultimately driving long-term success.

Balancing Costs with Employee Satisfaction

Balancing costs with employee satisfaction is a critical challenge for businesses aiming to optimize their expenses while maintaining a motivated workforce. As organizations strive to enhance productivity, the pressure to reduce costs can lead to decisions that negatively impact employee morale and engagement. It is essential to adopt strategies that not only focus on financial outcomes but also recognize the importance of creating a positive work environment. By aligning cost management practices with employee satisfaction, companies can cultivate a culture that promotes both efficiency and well-being.

One effective approach to achieving this balance is through flexible work arrangements. The rise of remote work has demonstrated that employees value the ability to manage their schedules and work environments. Companies that embrace flexible policies can reduce overhead costs associated with physical office spaces while simultaneously increasing employee satisfaction. Research shows that when employees have more control over their work-life balance, their productivity often improves, leading to better overall performance. This dual benefit makes flexible arrangements a strategic choice for cost-conscious organizations.

Investing in employee training and development also plays a crucial role in balancing costs with satisfaction. While training programs require upfront investment, they yield significant returns in the form of enhanced skills, improved performance, and increased employee retention. Organizations that prioritize development opportunities demonstrate a commitment to their workforce, fostering loyalty and reducing turnover costs. By viewing training as a strategic investment rather than an expense, businesses can enhance employee engagement while simultaneously building a more competent and efficient team.

Technology solutions offer another avenue for managing costs without sacrificing employee satisfaction. Implementing tools for performance metrics and cost efficiency can streamline operations and empower employees to contribute to the organization's financial goals. For instance, utilizing data analytics can help identify areas where costs can be minimized while maintaining or enhancing productivity. Furthermore, technology can facilitate better communication and collaboration among remote teams, ensuring that employees feel connected and valued, regardless of their physical location.

Lastly, cultivating a culture of cost awareness among employees is vital for long-term success. When employees understand the financial implications of their roles and decisions, they are more likely to engage in practices that support the organization's cost-saving initiatives. This can be achieved through transparent communication about financial goals and encouraging input from employees on cost management strategies. By fostering an environment where employees feel responsible for both their performance and the organization's financial health, businesses can create a more engaged workforce that contributes to both employee satisfaction and overall cost efficiency.

Chapter 7: Performance Metrics for Cost Efficiency

Key Performance Indicators for Cost Management

Key Performance Indicators (KPIs) for cost management are essential tools for businesses aiming to enhance productivity while simultaneously reducing expenses. In the context of employee cost management, these indicators provide measurable values that help business leaders evaluate the efficiency of their workforce and the effectiveness of their cost-related strategies. By carefully selecting and monitoring relevant KPIs, companies can identify areas for improvement, optimize resource allocation, and ensure that their financial goals align with their operational objectives.

One of the primary KPIs to consider is the Cost Per Hire, which quantifies the total expenditure involved in recruiting new employees. This metric encompasses various expenses, including advertising, recruitment agency fees, and onboarding costs. By analyzing the Cost Per Hire, organizations can assess the effectiveness of their recruitment strategies and make informed decisions about whether to invest in outsourcing recruitment or to develop in-house capabilities. A lower Cost Per Hire may indicate a more efficient hiring process, while a higher cost could prompt a re-evaluation of recruitment methods.

Another critical KPI is Employee Productivity, often measured through output per labor hour or revenue per employee. This metric directly correlates with cost management as it indicates how effectively the workforce contributes to the organization's goals. By tracking productivity levels, businesses can identify high-performing teams or individuals and replicate successful practices across the organization. Additionally, fluctuations in productivity can signal the need for targeted employee training and development programs, which can enhance skills and ultimately improve performance without significantly increasing costs.

Employee Turnover Rate serves as a vital KPI that reflects the organization's ability to retain talent. High turnover can lead to increased recruitment and training expenses, which undermine cost management efforts. By monitoring this KPI, businesses can implement strategies aimed at improving employee engagement and retention. Creating a culture of cost awareness among employees, along with offering competitive benefits and compensation packages, can significantly contribute to reduced turnover and its associated costs, ensuring a more stable workforce.

Finally, the Return on Investment (ROI) from employee training and development initiatives is another key performance indicator that organizations must consider. This metric assesses the financial return on investments made in employee development programs compared to the costs incurred. By evaluating the ROI, businesses can determine the effectiveness of their training efforts and make data-driven decisions about future investments in employee development. A strong ROI indicates that training programs are enhancing employee capabilities, leading to increased productivity and reduced operational costs.

In conclusion, effective cost management in employee-related strategies hinges on the careful selection and monitoring of relevant KPIs. By focusing on metrics such as Cost Per Hire, Employee Productivity, Employee Turnover Rate, and Training ROI, businesses can enhance their operations, improve decision-making processes, and ultimately achieve a more efficient and cost-effective workforce. Emphasizing these KPIs not only aids in financial management but also fosters a culture of continuous improvement within the organization, driving long-term success in a competitive business landscape.

Analyzing Employee Performance Data

Analyzing employee performance data is a critical component in the quest for efficient employee cost management. By systematically evaluating performance metrics, businesses can identify areas where productivity can be enhanced while simultaneously managing expenses. This analysis involves not only looking at quantitative metrics, such as sales figures or project completion rates, but also qualitative data that provides insight into employee engagement and effectiveness. Integrating these diverse data points allows organizations to create a comprehensive picture of employee performance, which is essential for informed decision-making.

One of the primary advantages of analyzing performance data is the ability to pinpoint high-performing employees and teams. Understanding what drives their success can inform training and development programs, allowing organizations to replicate effective practices across the workforce. This approach not only boosts overall productivity but also enhances the return on investment for employee training initiatives. By focusing resources on proven strategies, businesses can minimize unnecessary expenditures while maximizing employee output.

In the context of remote work, performance data analysis becomes even more critical. With many employees working from home, traditional oversight methods are less applicable, making it essential to rely on data-driven insights. Metrics such as project timelines, communication frequency, and output quality can help identify potential issues before they escalate. Additionally, analyzing these data points can inform strategies for optimizing remote work costs by revealing which employees thrive in this environment and which may require additional support or adjustments in their work arrangements.

Furthermore, a thorough analysis of performance data facilitates a deeper understanding of the financial implications of employee engagement and retention strategies. Engaged employees are typically more productive and less likely to leave the organization, which can significantly reduce turnover costs. By assessing employee performance alongside engagement metrics, businesses can develop targeted initiatives that foster a culture of cost awareness and accountability among employees, driving both satisfaction and productivity.

Lastly, the integration of technology solutions for performance data analysis enhances the efficiency of these processes. Advanced software can streamline data collection and analysis, providing real-time insights that drive timely decision-making. Implementing these technological tools not only reduces the time and cost associated with manual data analysis but also equips managers with the information they need to optimize staffing strategies, whether through outsourcing or in-house recruitment. As organizations strive to enhance productivity while reducing expenses, the strategic analysis of employee performance data will remain a cornerstone of effective cost management practices.

Using Metrics for Continuous Improvement

Using metrics for continuous improvement in employee cost management is essential for businesses seeking to enhance productivity while simultaneously reducing expenses. Metrics provide a tangible way to measure performance, identify inefficiencies, and track progress over time. By establishing key performance indicators (KPIs) tailored to specific business goals, organizations can gain insights into where resources are being effectively utilized and where adjustments may be necessary. This data-driven approach allows businesses to respond proactively to challenges and capitalize on opportunities for improvement.

In the context of remote work cost optimization, metrics such as employee productivity rates, project completion timelines, and communication efficiency can be invaluable. Analyzing these metrics helps organizations understand the impact of remote work on overall performance. For instance, if productivity metrics indicate a decline during remote work phases, businesses can explore solutions such as enhanced training or improved technology tools to support employees better. This continuous feedback loop enables organizations to make informed decisions that align with their operational goals while managing costs effectively.

Employee training and development ROI is another critical area where metrics can drive continuous improvement. By tracking training costs against employee performance post-training, businesses can evaluate the effectiveness of their programs. Metrics such as employee retention rates, promotion rates, and productivity improvements can quantify the value derived from training investments. This evaluation not only justifies the costs associated with training but also highlights areas for enhancement, ensuring that future training initiatives are more aligned with employee needs and organizational objectives.

Technology solutions for cost management also benefit significantly from a metrics-driven approach. By measuring the efficiency and effectiveness of various technology tools employed within the organization, businesses can identify which solutions provide the best return on investment. Metrics related to software usage, integration effectiveness, and time saved through automation can reveal opportunities for further streamlining processes. Organizations can leverage these insights to phase out underperforming technologies and invest in more impactful solutions, ultimately leading to better cost management.

Lastly, fostering a culture of cost awareness among employees is crucial to sustaining continuous improvement in cost management. Encouraging employees to engage with performance metrics not only promotes transparency but also empowers them to take ownership of their contributions toward cost efficiency. Regular communication of relevant metrics and their implications can motivate employees to adopt more cost-effective behaviors. By embedding this mindset into the organizational culture, businesses can cultivate an environment where every team member actively participates in identifying cost-saving opportunities, driving the overall success of employee cost management strategies.

Chapter 8: Outsourcing vs. In-House Staffing Strategies

Cost Analysis of Outsourcing

Cost analysis of outsourcing is a critical component for businesses considering this strategy as a means to enhance productivity while managing expenses. Outsourcing can offer significant cost savings by transferring specific functions to external vendors who specialize in those areas. This allows companies to focus on their core competencies while leveraging the expertise of third-party providers. However, a thorough cost analysis is essential to understand the implications of outsourcing, including hidden costs that may not be immediately apparent.

One key aspect of cost analysis in outsourcing is evaluating the direct costs versus potential savings. Direct costs include the fees paid to the outsourced vendor, which can often appear lower than maintaining in-house staff due to savings on salaries, benefits, and overhead. However, businesses must also account for indirect costs such as the time spent on vendor management, potential quality control issues, and the risk of service disruptions. A comprehensive analysis will help identify whether the savings truly outweigh the costs involved.

Another critical factor to consider is the impact of outsourcing on employee training and development. While outsourcing may reduce immediate labor costs, it can create gaps in knowledge and skills within the organization. Companies must assess the long-term return on investment (ROI) of employee training programs that could be affected by outsourcing decisions. The cost analysis should include potential expenses related to retraining employees, onboarding new staff, and the risk of losing institutional knowledge, which can ultimately affect productivity.

Technology solutions also play a significant role in the cost analysis of outsourcing. The integration of technology can enhance communication and streamline processes between businesses and outsourced providers. However, there may be additional costs associated with implementing new technology systems or upgrading existing ones to facilitate this collaboration. A careful evaluation of these technology-related expenses, alongside the anticipated efficiency gains, is necessary to produce a balanced cost analysis that accurately reflects the financial impact of outsourcing decisions.

Lastly, businesses must consider the broader implications of outsourcing on employee engagement and retention. Outsourcing can lead to a shift in company culture, potentially affecting employee morale and loyalty. The cost analysis should incorporate factors such as the potential decrease in employee satisfaction and the associated costs of turnover, which can be significant. By evaluating these elements, organizations can make informed decisions that align their outsourcing strategies with their overall goals for enhancing productivity while maintaining a cost-effective workforce.

Benefits of In-House Staffing

In-house staffing offers several advantages that can significantly enhance productivity while simultaneously reducing expenses. One of the primary benefits is the ability to cultivate a deep understanding of the company culture and values among employees. When staff members are integrated into the organization, they are more likely to align their efforts with the company's goals. This alignment fosters a sense of ownership and commitment, which can lead to increased motivation and enhanced performance. Moreover, in-house teams can communicate more effectively, reducing the chances of misunderstandings and errors that often occur in remote or outsourced environments.

Another key benefit of in-house staffing is the enhanced control over training and development. Organizations can tailor training programs to meet specific needs, ensuring that employees acquire skills that are directly relevant to their roles. This focused approach not only maximizes the return on investment for training expenditures but also helps in building a more competent workforce. Employees benefit from ongoing development opportunities, which can lead to greater job satisfaction and retention. When employees see that their employer is invested in their professional growth, they are more likely to remain engaged and committed to the organization.

In-house teams can also facilitate more efficient performance metrics and monitoring. By having employees on-site, managers can observe workflows, provide immediate feedback, and implement changes as necessary. This real-time oversight allows for the identification of inefficiencies and areas for improvement, ultimately driving cost savings. Additionally, in-house staff can collaborate more seamlessly on projects, leading to higher quality outcomes and reduced time spent on revisions or corrections. The ability to monitor performance closely contributes to a culture of accountability and continuous improvement.

The financial implications of in-house staffing extend beyond direct salary costs. While it may seem that outsourcing can provide short-term savings, hidden costs often arise from miscommunication, delays, and lower quality work. In-house staffing minimizes these risks, as employees are more familiar with the company's processes and expectations. Furthermore, in-house teams can leverage existing technology solutions effectively, optimizing tools that have already been integrated into the organization. This synergy between staff and technology not only reduces operational costs but also enhances overall productivity.

Lastly, in-house staffing can lead to stronger employee engagement and retention strategies. When employees feel a sense of belonging and connection to their workplace, they are less likely to seek opportunities elsewhere. This stability translates into lower recruitment and training costs, as well as a more experienced and cohesive workforce. A focused approach to employee engagement fosters loyalty and advocacy for the company, creating a positive cycle that reinforces both performance and cost management. By investing in their in-house teams, organizations can build a resilient workforce capable of driving sustainable success.

Decision-Making Framework for Staffing

A structured decision-making framework for staffing is essential for organizations aiming to enhance productivity while managing employee costs effectively. This framework should encompass several critical components, including clear objectives, data-driven analysis, stakeholder involvement, and a systematic approach to evaluating options. By establishing well-defined objectives, businesses can align their staffing strategies with their overall goals, ensuring that each hiring decision contributes to the organization's success in a measurable way.

Data-driven analysis is a cornerstone of effective decision-making in staffing. Organizations should leverage performance metrics that assess both current workforce effectiveness and projected needs based on market trends and business forecasts. Tools such as workforce analytics can provide insights into employee performance, turnover rates, and skill gaps, enabling businesses to make informed decisions regarding hiring, training, and development. By employing these analytical tools, companies can identify areas where cost efficiencies can be achieved, such as optimizing the mix of full-time employees and part-time or contract workers.

Stakeholder involvement is another crucial element in the staffing decision-making framework. Engaging managers, team leaders, and employees in the process ensures that multiple perspectives are considered, fostering a culture of collaboration and shared responsibility. This approach not only enhances the quality of the decision-making process but also improves employee engagement and retention, as staff members feel valued and included in the organization's strategic direction. Moreover, obtaining input from various levels can reveal insights into operational challenges and opportunities that might otherwise be overlooked.

Evaluating options systematically is vital for making sound staffing decisions. Organizations should develop criteria for assessing potential hires or staffing solutions based on factors such as cost, skill alignment, cultural fit, and potential for growth. This evaluation should also consider the implications of flexible work arrangements, remote work, and outsourcing versus in-house staffing strategies. By weighing these options against established criteria, businesses can identify the most efficient and effective staffing solutions that align with their cost management goals.

Finally, fostering a culture of cost awareness among employees is integral to the success of any staffing strategy. When employees understand the financial impacts of their roles and the importance of efficient resource utilization, they are more likely to contribute to cost-saving initiatives. Organizations can support this culture through regular training and development programs that emphasize the significance of cost management. Additionally, establishing clear communication about budget constraints and performance expectations can empower employees to make decisions that support the company's financial objectives while enhancing overall productivity.

Chapter 9: Employee Engagement and Retention Cost Strategies

Assessing Employee Engagement Levels

Assessing employee engagement levels is crucial for organizations aiming to enhance productivity while managing costs effectively. High levels of engagement correlate with increased productivity, reduced turnover, and greater employee satisfaction. To assess these levels, businesses can employ a variety of methods, including surveys, one-on-one interviews, and focus groups. These tools can provide insight into how employees feel about their roles, the company's culture, and their overall job satisfaction. Understanding these factors not only aids in identifying areas for improvement but also highlights what is working well within the organization.

Surveys are one of the most effective ways to gauge employee engagement. A well-crafted survey can uncover insights into employees' feelings about their work environment, management practices, and opportunities for growth. Questions should focus on key areas such as job satisfaction, alignment with company goals, and perceived support from leadership. By analyzing survey results, businesses can identify trends and specific issues that may be impacting engagement levels. Regularly conducting these surveys allows for tracking changes over time and assessing the impact of any initiatives implemented to improve engagement.

In addition to surveys, qualitative assessments through one-on-one interviews and focus groups can provide deeper insights into employee sentiments. These methods allow employees to express their thoughts in a more open manner, often revealing nuances that numbers alone cannot capture. Engaging in dialogue with employees can also foster a sense of value and belonging within the organization. By understanding the reasons behind employee engagement levels, businesses can tailor their strategies to address specific concerns and reinforce positive aspects of the workplace culture.

Technology can play a significant role in assessing and enhancing employee engagement. Platforms that facilitate real-time feedback and communication can provide ongoing insights into employee sentiments. Additionally, data analytics tools can help organizations track engagement metrics over time, allowing for more informed decision-making. By leveraging technology, businesses can not only assess engagement levels more efficiently but also implement solutions that promote ongoing engagement, such as training programs, recognition initiatives, and flexible work arrangements.

Ultimately, assessing employee engagement levels should be seen as an ongoing process rather than a one-time evaluation. By fostering a culture of continuous feedback and open communication, organizations can create an environment where employees feel valued and motivated. This, in turn, leads to higher retention rates and more effective cost management strategies. By understanding the dynamics of employee engagement, businesses can streamline their operations and ensure that their workforce is aligned with the organization's goals, ultimately driving success in a competitive landscape.

Cost-Benefit Analysis of Retention Strategies

Cost-benefit analysis of retention strategies is a critical tool for businesses seeking to enhance productivity while managing expenses effectively. Retention strategies, which encompass various initiatives aimed at keeping employees engaged and satisfied, can lead to significant financial implications for organizations. By evaluating the costs associated with implementing these strategies against the potential benefits, businesses can make informed decisions that align with their goals of efficient employee cost management. This analysis is particularly vital in the context of remote work optimization, where companies must balance the expenses of technology and training with the retention of top talent.

One of the key components of cost-benefit analysis in retention strategies is understanding the direct and indirect costs involved.

Direct costs may include salaries, benefits, and expenses related to training and development programs aimed at improving employee skills. Indirect costs, however, often encompass the impact of employee turnover, which can include recruitment expenses, lost productivity, and diminished morale among remaining staff. By quantifying these costs, businesses can better appreciate the financial impact that retention strategies can have on their overall bottom line.

The benefits of effective retention strategies extend beyond mere cost savings. Engaged employees tend to exhibit higher productivity levels, which can lead to increased output and improved quality of work. Furthermore, a well-implemented retention strategy can enhance the organization's reputation, making it easier to attract top talent in the future. This is particularly important in a competitive job market where skilled professionals are in high demand. The positive effects of retention on company culture and employee morale can also contribute to a more cohesive and motivated workforce, ultimately translating to better financial performance.

Technology solutions play a pivotal role in executing cost-effective retention strategies. Businesses can leverage data analytics to monitor employee engagement, identify at-risk employees, and tailor retention efforts accordingly. These technological tools can also streamline training and development processes, ensuring that employees receive the support they need without incurring excessive costs. By investing in the right technology, organizations can significantly improve their ability to retain employees while minimizing the financial burden associated with high turnover rates.

In conclusion, the cost-benefit analysis of retention strategies is essential for businesses aiming to optimize their workforce management while controlling expenses. By carefully evaluating the costs associated with retention initiatives against the tangible benefits they bring, organizations can develop a clear understanding of the financial implications. This insight enables businesses to make strategic decisions that enhance employee engagement, productivity, and ultimately, their overall financial health. As companies navigate the complexities of employee cost management, prioritizing retention through informed analysis will be a vital component of sustainable success.

Building a Culture of Engagement

Building a culture of engagement within an organization is essential for driving productivity while simultaneously managing employee costs effectively. Engaged employees are more likely to demonstrate higher levels of commitment, creativity, and performance, which can lead to significant cost savings and enhanced operational efficiency. To foster this culture, business leaders must prioritize open communication, recognition, and opportunities for growth. By doing so, they not only create a more pleasant work environment but also ensure that employees feel valued and connected to the organization's goals.

One of the foundational elements of an engaging workplace is transparent communication. Organizations should establish clear channels for sharing information about company objectives, performance metrics, and individual contributions. Regular updates and feedback sessions can help employees understand how their roles directly impact the company's success. When employees are aware of the bigger picture, they are more likely to align their efforts with organizational goals, leading to improved productivity and reduced turnover costs.

Recognition is another critical component of an engaging culture. Acknowledging employee achievements, whether through formal awards or informal shout-outs, can significantly boost morale. When employees feel appreciated for their contributions, they are more motivated to maintain high performance levels. This can result in lower recruitment and training expenses, as retaining skilled employees is often more cost-effective than constantly bringing in new talent. Incorporating recognition programs into the company culture can create a sense of belonging and loyalty among employees, further enhancing engagement.

Investing in employee training and development is a strategic approach that yields substantial returns on investment. Providing opportunities for professional growth not only equips employees with the skills necessary to excel in their roles but also demonstrates the organization's commitment to their personal and career advancement. This investment enhances productivity and fosters loyalty, reducing the likelihood of turnover. Moreover, a well-trained workforce can adapt more readily to changes in the marketplace, making the organization more resilient and cost-efficient in the long run.

To effectively build a culture of engagement, organizations must also leverage technology solutions that facilitate collaboration and communication, especially in remote work environments. Utilizing tools that promote teamwork and streamline processes can enhance employee satisfaction and productivity. Additionally, flexible work arrangements can cater to diverse employee needs, further boosting engagement while optimizing costs. By creating an inclusive environment where employees feel empowered to contribute, organizations can cultivate a culture of cost awareness that not only benefits the bottom line but also drives sustainable growth.

Chapter 10: Flexible Work Arrangements and Financial Impact

Benefits of Flexible Work Policies

Flexible work policies have emerged as a pivotal element in modern business strategies, particularly in the context of enhancing productivity while managing employee costs. These policies, which include options such as remote work, flexible hours, and hybrid work models, enable organizations to adapt to the diverse needs of their workforce. By allowing employees to tailor their work schedules and environments, businesses can foster a more engaged and motivated workforce, which is essential for driving productivity. The positive correlation between employee satisfaction and performance underscores the importance of implementing flexible work arrangements that align with the evolving expectations of today's employees.

One of the primary benefits of flexible work policies is the potential for significant cost savings. Organizations can reduce overhead expenses related to office space, utilities, and supplies when employees work remotely or on flexible schedules. This reduction in physical workspace requirements not only lowers direct costs but also allows businesses to allocate resources more strategically. By optimizing space usage, companies can invest in technology solutions that enhance remote work capabilities, ultimately leading to improved operational efficiency and a better return on investment in employee training and development.

Moreover, flexible work arrangements can enhance employee retention and engagement, two critical factors in managing workforce costs. When employees feel empowered to manage their own schedules, they are more likely to experience job satisfaction and loyalty to their employer. This heightened engagement translates into lower turnover rates, which can be particularly costly for businesses. The expenses associated with recruiting, onboarding, and training new employees can quickly add up, making it essential for organizations to prioritize retention strategies that include flexible work options.

In addition to improving retention, flexible work policies can also positively impact performance metrics related to cost efficiency. By enabling employees to work in environments where they feel most productive, organizations can see an increase in output quality and quantity. This outcome is particularly relevant in knowledge-based industries, where the ability to focus without the distractions of a traditional office can lead to enhanced innovation and problem-solving capabilities. As companies track performance metrics, they can gain insights into how flexible work arrangements contribute to overall success and cost management efforts.

Finally, fostering a culture of cost awareness among employees can be reinforced through flexible work policies. When employees are given the freedom to choose when and where they work, they also become more conscious of their contributions to the company's financial health. This awareness encourages them to seek out efficiencies in their work processes and collaborate more effectively with colleagues. By integrating flexible work arrangements into the broader context of workforce planning and budgeting techniques, businesses can create a sustainable model that not only enhances productivity but also supports long-term financial stability and growth.

Analyzing Cost Implications

Analyzing cost implications is a critical aspect of efficient employee cost management, particularly in today's dynamic business environment. Understanding the financial impact of various strategies allows businesses to make informed decisions that not only enhance productivity but also reduce expenses. It is essential for business leaders to dissect the cost structures associated with employee management, including salaries, benefits, training, and technology investments. By comprehensively assessing these elements, organizations can identify areas where they can streamline operations and allocate resources more effectively.

One significant area to analyze is the cost of remote work. As businesses increasingly adopt flexible work arrangements, understanding the implications of this shift on operational costs becomes paramount. Remote work can lead to reduced overhead expenses, such as office space and utilities, but it may also necessitate investments in technology and cybersecurity. By evaluating these factors, businesses can create a balanced approach that maximizes cost savings while ensuring employees remain productive and engaged in a remote environment.

Employee training and development represent another critical cost area that demands careful analysis. The return on investment (ROI) for training programs can vary significantly based on how they are structured and delivered. Organizations must assess not only the direct costs of training but also the long-term benefits, such as increased employee performance and retention. By quantifying these aspects, businesses can develop targeted training initiatives that yield higher returns, ultimately fostering a more skilled workforce while managing expenses effectively.

Technology solutions play a vital role in cost management strategies. Automating processes can lead to significant savings by reducing the need for manual labor and minimizing errors. However, the initial investment in technology must be weighed against potential long-term savings. A thorough cost-benefit analysis can help organizations determine the most suitable technological investments that align with their strategic goals. Furthermore, leveraging data analytics can provide insights into performance metrics, enabling businesses to pinpoint inefficiencies and optimize their workforce more effectively.

Lastly, fostering a culture of cost awareness among employees is crucial for sustainable employee cost management. When employees understand the financial implications of their roles and decisions, they are more likely to contribute to cost-saving initiatives. Implementing transparent communication about budgeting and expenses can empower employees to think critically about their work processes. By promoting engagement and retention strategies that align with cost management goals, organizations can create an environment where employees are motivated to contribute positively to the company's financial health while enhancing overall productivity.

Implementing Flexibility in a Cost-Effective Way

Implementing flexibility in the workplace is a crucial strategy for businesses seeking to enhance productivity while managing employee costs effectively. Flexibility can take many forms, including remote work arrangements, flexible hours, and job-sharing opportunities. These approaches not only cater to the diverse needs of employees but also create an environment where they can perform at their best. By aligning work arrangements with employee preferences, companies can foster a more engaged workforce, which in turn can lead to higher retention rates and reduced costs associated with turnover.

To implement flexibility cost-effectively, organizations must first assess their current operational structure and identify areas where flexibility can be introduced without compromising productivity. This assessment should include evaluating roles that can be performed remotely, understanding the technological requirements for effective remote work, and determining which employees would benefit most from flexible arrangements. By carefully selecting which positions can adapt to flexible work models, businesses can maintain efficiency while minimizing the potential disruption to workflows.

Investing in technology solutions is vital for facilitating flexible work arrangements. Tools that support collaboration, project management, and communication are essential for remote teams to function effectively. By leveraging cloud-based platforms and software, businesses can ensure that employees have access to the resources they need, regardless of their location. Moreover, these technologies often come with analytics features that allow organizations to monitor performance metrics, helping them evaluate the effectiveness of their flexible work strategies and make data-driven adjustments as necessary.

Employee training and development also play a critical role in successfully implementing flexibility. Providing training focused on time management, digital collaboration tools, and self-motivation can empower employees to thrive in a flexible environment. Furthermore, organizations should measure the return on investment (ROI) for these training initiatives to ensure that they contribute positively to overall employee performance and cost management. When employees feel equipped to handle the challenges of flexible work, their productivity is likely to increase, and the organization will benefit from reduced costs associated with inefficiency.

Finally, fostering a culture of cost awareness among employees is essential when implementing flexibility. Engaging employees in discussions about the financial implications of their work arrangements can lead to a better understanding of how their choices impact the organization's bottom line. Encouraging open communication about cost management and involving employees in decision-making processes can enhance their commitment to the company's financial goals. When employees recognize their role in driving efficiency, they are more likely to embrace flexible work arrangements that align with the organization's objectives, ultimately creating a more sustainable and cost-effective workplace.

Chapter 11: Workforce Planning and Budgeting Techniques

Strategic Workforce Planning

Strategic workforce planning is a critical process that aligns an organization's human capital strategy with its business goals, ensuring that the right people are in the right roles at the right times. This proactive approach not only enhances productivity but also optimizes employee cost management by anticipating future workforce needs based on market trends, business objectives, and technological advancements. By carefully analyzing workforce demographics, skills gaps, and the competitive landscape, businesses can make informed decisions that reduce expenses while maximizing the potential of their human resources.

In the context of remote work, strategic workforce planning takes on added complexity. Organizations must evaluate the cost implications of maintaining a remote workforce, including the need for technology solutions that support collaboration and productivity. By implementing effective remote work policies, businesses can minimize overhead costs while still providing employees with the tools they need to perform efficiently. Additionally, assessing the long-term viability of remote work arrangements allows companies to create flexible strategies that can adapt to changing market conditions without compromising employee engagement or performance.

Employee training and development are vital components of strategic workforce planning, as they directly contribute to the return on investment (ROI) for employee costs. By identifying skills shortages and investing in targeted training programs, organizations not only enhance employee capabilities but also improve retention rates and job satisfaction. This investment in human capital ensures that employees are equipped with the necessary skills to adapt to evolving business needs, ultimately driving productivity and reducing turnover-related expenses.

Performance metrics play a pivotal role in evaluating the effectiveness of workforce planning initiatives. By establishing clear performance indicators related to cost efficiency, organizations can gauge the impact of their strategic decisions on overall productivity and employee engagement. This data-driven approach enables businesses to identify areas for improvement and to make informed adjustments to their workforce strategies, ensuring that employee costs are managed effectively while still fostering a high-performance culture.

Finally, fostering a culture of cost awareness among employees is essential for successful strategic workforce planning. When employees understand the financial implications of their actions, they are more likely to engage in behaviors that support cost management initiatives. This cultural shift can be reinforced through transparent communication, regular training sessions, and performance incentives that align with the organization's financial goals. By creating an environment where employees are invested in cost optimization, businesses can enhance overall efficiency and drive sustainable growth.

Budgeting for Employee Costs

Budgeting for employee costs is a critical component in the overarching strategy for efficient employee cost management. As businesses navigate the complexities of workforce expenses, understanding the various components that contribute to employee costs is essential. This includes not only salaries and wages but also benefits, training, and other indirect costs. By creating a detailed budget that encompasses all aspects of employee expenditure, organizations can gain insight into their financial commitments and make informed decisions that enhance productivity while minimizing unnecessary expenses.

In the context of remote work, budgeting becomes particularly nuanced. Companies must account for the costs associated with technology, such as software licenses, virtual collaboration tools, and cybersecurity measures, which have become integral to supporting a remote workforce. Additionally, there are indirect costs related to employee well-being, including potential stipends for home office setups or internet reimbursements. A well-structured budget for remote work can lead to optimized costs, ensuring that the investment in technology and employee support translates into enhanced productivity and engagement.

Training and development represent another significant area in employee cost management. Organizations need to budget not just for the immediate costs of training programs but also for the long-term return on investment (ROI) that these initiatives can yield. By investing in employee development, businesses can foster a more skilled workforce that drives innovation and efficiency. A strategic approach to budgeting for training allows companies to align their learning and development initiatives with their overall business goals, ensuring that resources are allocated effectively and measurable outcomes are achieved.

Technology solutions play a vital role in employee cost management, and budgeting for these tools can lead to substantial savings. Implementing software that automates payroll, benefits administration, and performance tracking can reduce manual labor and minimize errors. Furthermore, leveraging data analytics can provide valuable insights into workforce performance and costs, allowing businesses to adjust their strategies proactively. By incorporating technology into the budgeting process, companies can streamline operations and enhance their ability to monitor and control employee costs.

Finally, fostering a culture of cost awareness among employees is crucial for effective budgeting. When employees understand the financial implications of their actions, they can contribute to cost-saving strategies. Encouraging open communication regarding financial goals and inviting employee input on cost management initiatives can lead to innovative solutions that benefit both the organization and its workforce. By integrating employee engagement into budgeting processes, businesses can create a collaborative approach to cost management that not only reduces expenses but also enhances overall morale and retention.

Forecasting Future Workforce Needs

Forecasting future workforce needs is a critical aspect of strategic planning for any organization aiming to optimize employee costs while enhancing productivity. As businesses navigate an increasingly dynamic landscape, understanding the potential shifts in workforce requirements allows leaders to make informed decisions regarding hiring, training, and resource allocation. Accurate forecasting helps anticipate changes in demand, technological advancements, and market trends that could impact staffing levels and roles.

To effectively forecast future workforce needs, organizations must first analyze historical data related to employee performance, turnover rates, and industry trends. This analysis serves as a foundation for identifying patterns that can inform staffing projections. Additionally, engaging with key stakeholders across various departments can provide valuable insights into upcoming projects or initiatives that may require adjustments in workforce size or skill sets. By incorporating qualitative and quantitative data, businesses can create a more comprehensive view of their future workforce landscape.

Another essential component of workforce forecasting is the consideration of remote work dynamics. The shift to remote and hybrid work models has fundamentally changed how organizations approach staffing and productivity. Leaders must evaluate the skills and resources necessary for remote teams to function effectively, as well as the cost implications of maintaining a distributed workforce. By embracing technology solutions that facilitate communication and collaboration, businesses can optimize remote work arrangements while managing related expenses.

Employee training and development also play a crucial role in workforce forecasting. As industries evolve, the demand for new skills increases, necessitating a proactive approach to employee development. Organizations should assess current skill gaps and forecast future training needs aligned with their strategic objectives. Investing in employee training not only enhances productivity but also improves retention rates, thereby reducing the costs associated with high turnover. A well-trained workforce is more adaptable and capable of meeting future challenges, making it a key element in cost management strategies.

Finally, fostering a culture of cost awareness among employees can significantly influence workforce forecasting outcomes. When employees understand the financial implications of their roles and decisions, they are more likely to contribute to cost-saving initiatives. Encouraging open communication about budgeting and resource allocation can lead to innovative ideas that drive efficiency. By integrating cost awareness into the organizational culture, businesses can ensure that all team members are aligned with the goal of optimizing employee costs while maintaining productivity, ultimately leading to sustained organizational success.

Chapter 12: Cultivating a Culture of Cost Awareness

Importance of Cost Awareness Among Employees

Cost awareness among employees is crucial for organizations aiming to enhance productivity while simultaneously reducing expenses. When employees understand the financial implications of their actions, they are more likely to make decisions that contribute to the company's overall efficiency. This awareness fosters a culture where every team member feels responsible for the organization's financial health, leading to more conscientious spending and resource allocation. By integrating cost awareness into the company culture, businesses can empower employees to take ownership of their roles, ensuring that cost management is a shared responsibility rather than a top-down directive.

One significant benefit of promoting cost awareness is its impact on remote work cost optimization. As organizations increasingly adopt flexible work arrangements, understanding the financial aspects of remote operations becomes critical. Employees who are aware of costs associated with their work-from-home setups—such as utilities, internet, and equipment—can make informed choices that minimize expenses. For example, if employees are educated about the costs of using certain technologies or services, they may opt for more economical solutions, thus reducing the overall expenditure for the organization while still maintaining productivity.

Investing in employee training and development also yields a substantial return on investment (ROI) when tied to cost awareness. Training programs that emphasize financial literacy can equip employees with the skills needed to assess and manage costs within their specific roles. This not only enhances their performance but also aligns their personal goals with the organization's financial objectives. When employees recognize how their contributions affect the bottom line, they are more likely to engage in continuous improvement practices, leading to increased efficiency and reduced operational waste.

Technology solutions for cost management play a vital role in fostering a culture of cost awareness. By implementing tools that provide real-time data on expenses and performance metrics, organizations can help employees understand the financial impact of their daily decisions. These tools can facilitate transparency and accountability, empowering employees to make data-driven choices that align with the company's financial goals. Additionally, leveraging technology can streamline communication about costs, ensuring that all team members are on the same page regarding budget constraints and financial expectations.

Lastly, effective benefits and compensation analysis hinges on employee cost awareness. When employees understand the value of their benefits relative to the costs incurred by the organization, they are more likely to appreciate their compensation packages. This awareness can enhance employee engagement and retention, as individuals feel more connected to the company's financial strategies. Moreover, by involving employees in discussions around flexible work arrangements and their financial impacts, organizations can cultivate a collaborative environment that prioritizes both employee satisfaction and cost efficiency.

Strategies for Encouraging Cost-Conscious Behavior

Encouraging cost-conscious behavior within an organization requires a multi-faceted approach that integrates various strategies tailored to the business environment. One effective strategy is to foster a culture of cost awareness among employees. This can be achieved by incorporating cost management into the company's core values and operational practices. Regular training sessions that focus on the importance of cost efficiency can empower employees to recognize how their actions impact the organization's financial health. By promoting transparency regarding financial goals and challenges, employees can feel more connected to the company's mission and motivated to align their behaviors with cost-saving initiatives.

Another key strategy is to implement performance metrics that track cost efficiency. Establishing clear performance indicators related to cost management can help employees understand their individual and team contributions to the bottom line. These metrics should be communicated effectively, making it easy for employees to see how their efforts contribute to overall cost savings. Additionally, recognizing and rewarding employees who meet or exceed these cost-saving targets can further incentivize a cost-conscious mindset throughout the organization. Performance-based incentives can drive engagement and instill a sense of ownership over financial outcomes.

Leveraging technology solutions can also enhance cost-conscious behavior. Implementing tools that provide insights into spending patterns and resource utilization enables employees to make informed decisions that align with cost-saving goals. For instance, budget tracking software can help teams monitor their expenses in real-time, allowing for immediate adjustments when necessary. By equipping employees with the right technological resources, organizations can facilitate a proactive approach to cost management, helping to identify areas where savings can be made without sacrificing productivity or quality.

In addition to technology, flexible work arrangements can play a significant role in cost optimization. By offering remote work options, companies can reduce overhead costs associated with office space and utilities. Furthermore, remote work can lead to increased employee satisfaction and retention, which ultimately drives down recruitment and training costs. Encouraging employees to adopt cost-effective practices in their remote work setup, such as minimizing energy use and optimizing their home office expenses, can further contribute to the organization's financial efficiency.

Lastly, comprehensive employee training and development programs should emphasize the return on investment (ROI) of cost management initiatives. Training that focuses on financial literacy and the implications of spending decisions can equip employees with the knowledge to make cost-effective choices in their day-to-day responsibilities. By demonstrating how their roles contribute to the overall financial success of the organization, employees are more likely to engage in behaviors that support cost-conscious practices. Ultimately, fostering an environment where cost management is prioritized and recognized as a collective responsibility will lead to sustainable financial growth and enhanced productivity.

Measuring the Impact of Cost Awareness Programs

Measuring the impact of cost awareness programs is essential for organizations aiming to enhance productivity while reducing expenses. These programs are designed to instill a sense of financial responsibility among employees, allowing them to recognize the direct correlation between their actions and the company's financial health. By implementing systematic metrics, businesses can evaluate the effectiveness of these initiatives, ensuring that they align with overall strategic objectives. Key performance indicators (KPIs) such as cost savings achieved, employee engagement levels, and productivity rates serve as fundamental tools in this evaluation process.

One of the primary metrics to consider is the quantifiable cost savings resulting from the implementation of cost awareness programs. Organizations can track reductions in operational costs, waste, and resource utilization before and after program initiation. By comparing these figures, businesses can ascertain the financial impact of their initiatives. Additionally, analyzing employee behavior changes, such as reduced expenditure in project budgets or more prudent resource management, can further illustrate the effectiveness of the programs.

Furthermore, employee engagement serves as another critical metric. Engaged employees are more likely to embrace cost awareness initiatives, leading to higher productivity levels and improved morale. Surveys and feedback mechanisms can be employed to gauge employee perceptions of the cost awareness programs and their relevance to daily operations. This feedback can then inform adjustments and enhancements, ensuring that the programs resonate with the workforce's needs and expectations.

Incorporating technology solutions can also facilitate the measurement of cost awareness programs. Utilizing data analytics tools allows organizations to track and analyze employee performance more effectively. These tools can provide insights into spending patterns, project efficiencies, and overall resource allocation, enabling businesses to identify trends and areas for improvement. Moreover, technology can streamline communication and training efforts, ensuring that employees receive consistent messaging about cost management practices.

Ultimately, the success of cost awareness programs hinges on a culture that promotes financial responsibility throughout the organization. By fostering an environment where employees feel empowered to contribute to cost-saving measures, businesses can create a sustainable model for efficiency. Regularly reviewing performance metrics and adjusting strategies based on outcomes will not only enhance the effectiveness of cost awareness initiatives but also reinforce the importance of financial prudence among all employees. This holistic approach ensures that cost management becomes an integral part of the organizational culture, driving long-term success.

Chapter 13: Conclusion and Future Trends in Employee Cost Management

Summary of Key Strategies

In the landscape of modern business, effective employee cost management is crucial for maintaining profitability while fostering a productive work environment. A summary of key strategies reveals a multifaceted approach that balances cost reduction with enhanced employee engagement and productivity. Central to this approach is the adoption of remote work cost optimization. By leveraging technology to facilitate flexible work arrangements, businesses can reduce overhead costs associated with physical office spaces while empowering employees with the autonomy to balance their work and personal lives. This strategy not only minimizes expenses but also enhances job satisfaction, which can lead to improved retention rates.

Investing in employee training and development is another essential strategy that yields a strong return on investment. Companies that prioritize continuous learning and skill development see increased productivity as employees become more proficient in their roles. Additionally, a well-trained workforce can adapt more readily to technological changes and shifting market demands. To maximize the effectiveness of training programs, businesses should implement performance metrics that assess the impact of training on employee output and overall company performance. This data-driven approach allows for ongoing adjustments to training initiatives, ensuring that resources are allocated efficiently.

Technology solutions play a pivotal role in streamlining employee cost management. Implementing software for payroll processing, benefits administration, and performance tracking can significantly reduce administrative burdens and human error. Moreover, data analytics tools provide insights into employee performance and cost drivers, enabling organizations to make informed decisions. Investing in technology not only enhances operational efficiency but also positions companies to respond swiftly to economic changes, ultimately supporting a culture of cost awareness among employees.

The analysis of benefits and compensation is crucial for ensuring that employee remuneration aligns with market standards while remaining sustainable for the business. Conducting regular compensation reviews can help identify any discrepancies that may lead to employee dissatisfaction or turnover. Furthermore, a strategic approach to outsourcing versus in-house staffing can provide additional cost savings. Businesses should carefully evaluate their core competencies and consider outsourcing non-essential functions to specialized firms, allowing internal teams to focus on strategic initiatives that drive growth.

Finally, fostering employee engagement and retention through transparent communication and recognition programs can significantly reduce costs associated with turnover. Engaged employees are more likely to contribute positively to the company culture and productivity levels. Implementing flexible work arrangements, such as hybrid work models, can further enhance employee satisfaction while also being financially advantageous. By adopting these key strategies, businesses can create a robust framework for efficient employee cost management that not only supports financial objectives but also nurtures a motivated and skilled workforce.

Emerging Trends in Cost Management

Emerging trends in cost management reflect the evolving landscape of business practices, particularly in how organizations approach employee-related expenses. One significant trend is the shift towards remote work cost optimization. As more companies adopt hybrid or fully remote models, they face new challenges and opportunities in managing costs associated with employee productivity. Organizations are increasingly utilizing technology to monitor performance and streamline communication, ensuring that remote employees remain engaged and productive. This shift not only reduces overhead costs associated with physical office spaces but also necessitates a reevaluation of how companies budget for employee-related expenses, including home office stipends and technology reimbursements.

Another key trend is the focus on return on investment (ROI) for employee training and development. Businesses are recognizing that investing in their workforce leads to enhanced productivity and reduced turnover costs. By implementing data-driven training programs that align with company goals, organizations can measure the effectiveness of their investments in employee development. This approach allows for a more strategic allocation of resources, ensuring that training initiatives contribute directly to the bottom line. Furthermore, as the job market becomes increasingly competitive, companies that prioritize employee growth are likely to see improved retention rates, which can significantly lower recruitment and onboarding expenses.

Technology solutions for cost management are also gaining traction. Advanced analytics and software tools provide businesses with insights into spending patterns and employee performance metrics. These tools enable organizations to make informed decisions regarding employee compensation, benefits, and overall cost efficiency. By harnessing data, companies can identify areas of overspending and implement targeted strategies to reduce costs. Moreover, the integration of artificial intelligence in workforce management can streamline scheduling and resource allocation, further enhancing operational efficiency and minimizing wasteful expenditure.

The analysis of benefits and compensation is another crucial aspect of emerging cost management trends. Companies are increasingly scrutinizing their compensation packages to ensure they remain competitive while also being cost-effective. This involves not just salary considerations but also the evaluation of employee benefits, including health insurance and retirement plans. By adopting a holistic approach to compensation analysis, organizations can attract and retain top talent without compromising their financial health.

Additionally, flexible work arrangements are becoming essential, as they not only cater to employee preferences but can also lead to significant cost savings in terms of real estate and operational expenses.

Finally, fostering a culture of cost awareness among employees is emerging as a vital trend. Encouraging employees to take ownership of their spending and resource management can lead to a more efficient allocation of costs across the organization. This cultural shift involves training employees to understand the financial implications of their decisions and engage them in cost-saving initiatives. By promoting an environment where cost efficiency is a shared responsibility, companies can enhance employee engagement and retention while simultaneously optimizing their overall expenditures. As these trends continue to develop, organizations that adapt effectively will be well-positioned to achieve sustainable growth and profitability.

Preparing for the Future of Work

Preparing for the Future of Work requires a multifaceted approach that reflects the evolving landscape of business operations. As organizations increasingly adapt to trends such as remote work and technological advancement, it becomes essential to streamline employee cost management while enhancing productivity. Companies must focus on integrating cost-effective strategies that not only address current needs but also anticipate future challenges in the labor market. This proactive mindset will enable businesses to remain competitive while optimizing their workforce resources.

One key strategy for preparing for the future of work is to implement remote work cost optimization practices. As remote work becomes a permanent fixture in many industries, organizations need to assess the associated costs and benefits. By analyzing overhead expenses, technology requirements, and employee productivity metrics, businesses can identify areas for cost savings. Embracing digital collaboration tools and flexible work arrangements not only reduces physical office costs but also fosters a more adaptable workforce that can respond to market changes.

Training and development play a critical role in maximizing the return on investment (ROI) for employee expenditures. Investing in employee training ensures that the workforce remains skilled and competitive, which is vital in a rapidly changing job environment. Companies should focus on continuous learning initiatives that align with their strategic goals. By measuring the effectiveness of these programs through performance metrics, organizations can ensure that their training investments lead to increased productivity and reduced turnover, ultimately enhancing their bottom line.

Technology solutions are another essential element in preparing for the future of work. Leveraging advanced software and automation tools can streamline operational processes, reducing the need for excessive staffing and lowering operational costs. By adopting data-driven technologies, businesses can gain insights into employee performance and engagement, allowing for more informed decision-making regarding compensation and benefits. Additionally, integrating technology can facilitate better communication and collaboration among remote teams, further enhancing efficiency.

Lastly, cultivating a culture of cost awareness among employees is crucial for sustainable growth. Engaging employees in cost management initiatives fosters a sense of ownership and responsibility toward the organization's financial health. Providing training on financial literacy, incentivizing cost-saving suggestions, and involving teams in budgeting processes can instill a mindset that values efficiency. By aligning employee goals with the organization's cost management strategies, businesses can enhance engagement and retention while effectively preparing for the future landscape of work.

www.ingramcontent.com/pod-product-compliance
Lightning Source LLC
Chambersburg PA
CBHW070129230526
45472CB00004B/1481